REQUEENING

REQUEENING

POEMS

AMANDA MOORE

An Imprint of HarperCollins*Publishers*

HarperCollins books may be purchased for educational, business, or sales promotional use. For information, please email the Special Markets Department at SPsales@harpercollins.com.

Ecco® and HarperCollins® are trademarks of HarperCollins Publishers.

FIRST EDITION

Designed by Paula Russell Szafranski

Library of Congress Cataloging-in-Publication Data has been applied for.

ISBN 978-0-06-309628-8

21 22 23 24 25 LSC 10 9 8 7 6 5 4 3 2 1

FOR NATE AND CLEMENTINE

CONTENTS

REQUEENING

I stand in a column

Of winged, unmiraculous women,
Honey-drudgers.
I am no drudge

—SYLVIA PLATH, "STINGS"

Opening the Hive

Late afternoon slants, illuminates
the worn, white husk of hive and gleams
like an incubator bulb on the oval of an egg.
This might have been the way I was born
to move over my mother and wash from her
what was left of painful birth, her legs
like the old wood cracked with a hive tool,
my lips clamping and the bees burrowing
into honeycomb, bathed in sweetness,
a taste fresher when robbed this way.

Smoke to calm, to push the heaving down,
down to the center where the queen hides
and is stroked, flanked by the upturned rumps
of guard bees, wings fanning scent in warning.

I open this small universe and set it in motion,
a new heart ready to be fed and broken and fed again,
gathering strength to reseal and take into itself

what we leave behind: fingerprints
through broken comb and crushed drones.

This might have been the way I was born
then set to life: stolen honey clinging

to light hair that covers everything new.
Like late afternoon sunlight, a kiss
on my dented forehead, mother collapsed and emptied

of poison, barbed stinger, and the baby, the jelly, the bee.

1729 Maple Avenue Northbrook IL

gone the marriage the father gone
the plum tree out front its wild confetti
steady shade and sticky fruit blotching the sidewalk

gone the fence we'd be set to paint once a year
white droplets sprinkling the hostas
black house numbers trailing down the upright pole

the birch tree and its paper scrolls the slap
of the side door on its ancient hinge
the hook-and-eye lock gone

the limestone gravel drive my sister's
and my sock-tender feet callousing each summer
as we dared one another to race across gone

the garage its detritus and stash in the rafters
gone the radiant heat hot spots on the floor
the pull-down stairs to the attic and its boxes

old clothes in steam-weak cardboard
and crumbled bags gone the window unit AC
that kept one bedroom frigid while the rest

of the house sweltered and swooned
and the furniture we lugged
from room to room always remaking

gone the many couches and the weights
they held the transom windows and their cranks
the big bay that once collapsed

beneath a roof of half-melted snow
gone the dishwasher rolled out from the pantry
to hook to the sink skinnying around it on tiptoes

to reach the stove gone the white phone
anchored to the kitchen wall and who we called on it
gone the extra-long cord we would stretch

to reach our bedrooms the rubbery spirals
pulled tight gone the record player
and the VCR the CDs the DVDs the cable box

long gone the raspberry bush out back
my turned-up T-shirt bottom heavy
with fruit for breakfast

the jonquils and crocus that would shoulder through
snow-lashed dirt come spring gone the creek—
north branch of the Chicago River

that would swell some summers
tip over its banks gone the plans to ford it
or to build a bridge gone the single mother

her blue eye shadow silk blouses sour smell of nylons hot
in pointy shoes gone her gentle nature
and her rages too gone the grandmother

afternoon visits her handbags and bridge mix
gone her magic and unwanted advice
the joy the strife the nesting dolls we were

gone the death that wedged us open
the green in the windows
the wild the ordered harmony

and what we knew about the world then gone
the shelter women give one another
rough love flooding the house and yard

When I Hear "Horses" as "Corsets"

I imagine the great tethered body of my grandmother
galloping through tawny fields
beneath the last flame of a western sun
and admire the poet,
who I think is decrying the corset
for not being as fine or as real
as the form that moves beneath.

More and more these days
my eyes and ears collude
to make the world
more as I want it. I like this place,
where a team of corsets bends now
to drink from the river
and cool their sweat-lathered, satiny skins.

When I catch on at last,
the poet is nuzzling the neck of a real horse
that pulls back its thick, equine lips
and fogs her hand with grainy breath.

How magnificent, I think,
to nuzzle instead a corset, to curl
once more against my grandmother,
take in the powdery exhalations of her body,
run my fingertips across the bony spine
of the hook and eye seam,
press my cheek to the steely stays.

Hers is not a corset I will saddle and ride away,
and it might not take an apple from my hand,
but I'll fasten my small cart to it anyway.

Aunt Annie's Sand

I don't even know who Aunt Annie is,
how many *Greats* before her name
or which bronzed face is hers in tintype,
which side of which family she claimed:

spinster sister of someone else
long dead, leafless branch who left no one
with her name behind. I only know
about her sands the way I know

about the Arctic or the green flash at sunset:
a promise, a *someday-you'll-see-it*, someday
we'll park a giant green dumpster out front
and toss in the toaster boxes,

the crates of wire hangers,
moth-nibbled linens, bags
of canceled checks. And then
perhaps we'll find the bottles—

how many could there be? Blue,
brown, green, and clear beneath
their yellowed, peeling labels, sepia tilt
of cursive: *Salt Lake, New Jersey,*

Florida, all the places I imagine her
gathering her skirts to kneel
and collect, leaving voids
she thought too small

to notice—the sands her entry
in the messy record
my grandmother keeps: a family
in objects. All the things

and none of their stories: the deeds
we did to get them, what we kept
and what we stole, this past
we've made from pilfered dust.

Sonnet While Killing a Chicken

The most important thing a girl can learn
is how to kill a chicken for a meal
to feed a man, so she begins to turn
the bird by neck and bound feet—this skill real,
precise, my mother wringing damp bath towels
and snapping them on our rumps like the neck
snaps in the hand, wings sputter, bowels
release shit. The bird, its broken neck thick
with draining blood, is lowered to a tub
and bathed in scalding water. Feathers pulled
like flowers from roots. Feet sliced off. Wings nubbed
like new-formed breasts. The tenderest meat culled.
The chicken flat on its dead back. The knife
just above its neck. The girl. The first slice.

Waggle Dance

Everything beautiful can be reduced

      to scientific measurement:

this language

        this dance

     this swoop and waggle
across the hexagoned surface of comb

        twitter and figure eight
I watch through glass

at the observation hive.

        Some equation tracks

the angle of each figure   the number of times

       the bee swoops

       shakes wing-lit
       and crowded by her sisters

swoops again. We can follow the emergent

heroine and forager as she calculates

          tracks the distant food source.
It would take more than map
    to chart me
        my dips and spins

      my language. Who

could smell the flowers
       blooming inside: hibiscus

goldenrod and the tupelo tree?
Would my own sister know to track me?

Always more bee-like, virgin
and capped in her own little cell

she is as queenless as I
but trusts
the splintered walls of a sweet hive.

There are reasons we don't
all use the same tongue.

I prefer the mystery
of a bee's body returning

bright orange streaks of pollen
in the sacks on the backs of her legs

like fistfuls of hazy, polluted sun.

It doesn't matter

where she's been
or how long

she's been in flight,
her waggle familiar.

worlds buzz over us like bees,
we be splendid in new bones.
other people think they know
how long life is.
how strong life is.
we know.

—LUCILLE CLIFTON, "NEW BONES"

My Life Still with Wasps

I've lived in three homes in this town.
In three homes wasps
nestled my walls:

paper hives blooming wildly
unwanted August weeds.
They burrow toward my sleeping sounds at night

and in the day they track me
little sentinels from door
to driveway to door again.

The Bee Man arrives
to poison this new nest
and can only cross his fingers.

Once before they died in pools
along my porch. Another time
they chewed through wall and writhed

in inch-thick ribbons on my bed
until death gripped them in its teeth.
Once nestled a home cannot

cut wasps loose to life, send them flying
to wilder wider eaves,
abandoned house or hollow tree—

this isn't the mother's body, baby
breaking womb to emerge alive
and separate from what it fed upon.

A house swells with wasps
that will be carried out
only by death.

I am not afraid of such birth.

Which Came First

Attracted to her reckless laugh
that later made you cringe, the way she'd wait
each meal for you—wouldn't even eat
if you weren't there or on your way.
The body she revealed
a quarter at a time, never her full naked form:
girth of hips and soft, sweet rise of belly
that seemed to say she'd birth cherubs, roll out
sugar cookie children to melt across your tongue.

It was when she tried just that,
those pulpy messes and the doctors
looking right up between her legs.
It was when the temper she had turned like a torch
in the eyes of those in her way turned
on you, sneaking in the door late and guilty.

As teenagers, you would drive Illinois
back roads to drink beer, make out
and talk about the places you would travel.
All that corn might have looked like future
to the two of you, stretching and vast and topped
with the bit of silk you imagined life grew into.
When the farmers sow those seeds, they cast
so many that never root and grow. I wonder
how you never thought of that.

Ithaca

I know little of weaving
but that I can pull together
these strings of loneliness
and fashion some sort of shroud
to drape across my shelves.

The hills cradle my house
and my half-empty bed, but
I am no more a fixed point than love.

All night in bed I am unraveling.

They've built a highway outside my window.
Headlights trace my blank wall.

The moon is a wide-open O of pleasure.
My neighbors are making love.

Inertia in patience.

World of longing: people
will wait a long time for a hero.
I cannot expect to find him in my bed some night
pulling cobwebs from my hair.

I'm the one with a map.
My speedometer has a wise old face.

Foraging

The honey won't make itself, and so to the fields heavy with flower
        to pack pollen in the sacks of their legs
                load their stomachs with sweet nectar. Bees sustain

                the hive by taking flight and swarm that way too:
        lone messenger, tremor, and soon the queen
is gone. Some will follow, some will stay rooted

to the same honey-thick walls where a new queen
        will make her nuptial flight,
                small force of nature—a breeze

                that parts your hair or slides a scrap of paper through a crack
        in the floor. She will find the hive again after mating, grow
  too fat to fly, lay eggs for years, and never again

feel the sting of sun or ripple of wind off a drone's back.
        Instead, she births emissaries, little heralds of drought or storm
                to clean her with saliva they feed on faraway fields.

                These are the ways we taste the places we cannot see
        or touch, eat industry that isn't ours.
Drop the honey to your tongue. Taste these fields.

The Broken Leg

Eventually it comes between us:
not the plaster barricade
between every tender moment we might have,
but the dependence.

After the flurry of surgeons
and worry of permanent damage

there is the carrying of urine
changing of bandages
creak of crutches and incessant talk of scabs.

Like a shabby patch of grass
I am stretched out beneath him, trampled

and benignly offering servitude:
not the meal or the pillow, the TV or the bed or the Vicodin,
but the nagging truth behind it all.

In short, it's unromantic,

this child in the shape of my husband,
this outstretched hand, rumpled head and hungry mouth.
And the bright side? Well, talk to me another day.
For now it is logistics and medicine,
carpools and take-out pizza, not laughing
while he climbs the stairs on his butt.

And it's the weight of one house,
its dishes and litter and dust on my shoulders.

Then there is the moment
we look across the bed at one another,
mangled leg between us like a sleeping child,
and understand this is what long love will one day be:
a wheelchair, a diaper, a walker, forgetting

and then, for one of us, a solitude. For this glimpse
of how life will take us to our knees
before we leave it, I want to say

Thanks a lot.

It's hard enough some days
to drag myself from bed, tired pilgrim limping
toward the impossible grotto of happiness
without the truth so tangibly beside me:
this reminder of my body's tremendous capacity
for decay. And did I mention the servitude? How I proffer it
tenderly and resentfully at once, each day
a new opportunity to fail.

And yet, I don't despise the bike that broke his leg
and dragged us into knowing. At night
when I replay in dreams the afternoon
that flipped us both to the curb, sick wail of ambulance
and everything that followed, I don't always say *Stop.*

Don't be a jackass. You don't know what this will do to us.
Sometimes I say *Go faster. Let me see that trick you do again.*

Postern

Old car up on blocks.
Sides peeled back
expose undergirdings of door:
levers, pulleys, the secret pocket
where the window disappears
and a small galaxy of empty space—I thought

there would be more, something more solid
in this panel that separates me
from danger.

          I've always known
the cavern of engine block to be chock-full—
a puzzle of parts locked together, each one
solid, prominent in the way it needs
to be tweaked or filled or turned to jump.

But this door
          this floss I lean against:
mere metering arm, a deception
             sheathed in steel.

O the limits of safety
where we put our faith
what we allow to hold us.

While Killing Ants

As a child I thought we must look like them
from heaven: small, mysterious industry,
their strange conversations of scent. Parade
and shuttle and build—labor illogical,
inscrutable beneath an indifferent thumb.
My husband crushes and curses, but I
clean, redirect, try honey traps and orange oil,
borax in sugar, organic repellant:
I don't want to kill. They persist, seek
morsels farther back in the pantry, hold
our crumbs aloft, tracing their triumph home.
At last I agree to cast down poison—
my god: how quick it works, how smug the victor.
I am alone in the kitchen once more.

Anniversary Declaration

That there is a bed
the same shape as a calendar square—
each day begins and ends in it,
marks on a page.

That the bed
is the shape of windowpane, too,
pass-through and portal: transparent
and without privacy.

That the bed is a small box
and we a pair of earrings, tarnished
but bejeweled: cottoned together,
neither touching nor tangled.

Bed a field of flower
and grain, beauty that is
sustenance: romp and frolic
and play and seed.

Bed a field and scrimmage,
a boundary:
two teams
and for someone to win, the other—

Requeening

How familiar the sight of you in coveralls:
papery white and gliding between bees
safely—large moth, veil twittering behind
like a tattered old wing. How familiar
this part of summer: heavy, air

wringing each breath from our lungs
as we bend over hives that ooze honey
sharp and golden like afternoon's last rays of sun.

As I pump the smoker, you crack the hive,
pull out frames to inspect. We're working
our way down to the queen, checking brood,
how many cells turn with life:
it doesn't take long to see there aren't many.

How familiar your voice, how out of place
and I am irritated like the workers
returning with nectar, bright streaks of pollen
to find us poking through their ordered world.

                              She was the first queen
I spotted on the comb when I learned to tend hives
and now you say we should kill and replace her. I understand
she is not useful, can no longer produce
the brood to become the larvae to become the bee.

How many times I've opened your shirt at night
or taken down your pants and dreamed
of finding another body, new limbs, someone
with softer, darker hair—I am never surprised: your thumb,
her long thorax, the wake of workers stroking,
breathing her essence the way I breathe in yours.
I know you will crush her before I can argue.

There have been times I've wished you dead
for the new pureness of the grief I'd feel, but
I am overcome with different longing.

The hive will come to know the new, caged queen.
Her scent, alarming at first, will become
recognized, comforting. How familiar,
your shoulder beneath my hand: the way
you step away from the hive and out of the white suit.

Even if it would devour us, I would chew
through this cage we keep our love in
to make us new to each other once more.

None of the instincts will be hers that belong to a life of toil; she will have no brushes, no pockets wherein to secrete the wax, no baskets to gather the pollen. The habits, the passions, that we regard as inherent in the bee, will be all lacking in her. She will not crave for air, or the light of the sun; she will die without even once having tasted a flower.

—MAURICE MAETERLINCK, *THE LIFE OF THE BEE*

The Worker

Each cell tidy and tight with brood,
what's mine now
is sunshine and breeze

a gyre of pleasure and labor within.
I can carry it all:
crumb of flower, spittle and weight,

apple tree, blueberry,
what they need but don't want:
gloved hand or swab.

From a crack in concrete,
from weed
and bombshell I'll pull

nectar and sweet, a surplus
stacked neat and ready for plunder.
My flight even

is beauty and my churr in the air
the way I scatter beam
and your attention.

But I am tired of being the sting

of closing the door in winter
and sifting wing dust and limb
out front come spring.

I am vein in a seething heart of heat
a single platelet pumped
through the bright organ:

alone I canker and pique.
I don't want to be
vengeance, to see

in the world only what
I might yet forget to lance.
So I circle and comb,

tend brood, carry out
the dead, lead all
our voices to thrum.

20905 Caledonia Avenue Hazel Park MI

After tuning each floorboard
and scraping walls to chalky plaster

laying checkerboard tile and nailing
every shingle to the roof we made

a baby and I bore her in my body
until she broke me and we brought her there

where I milked myself each morning so happy
to make a home

for suffering, down to
the location even: the old place perched

on the edge of a city waking
from decades of cold dormancy.

I flinch with tenderness at the photos:
our young faces in undiscerning joy

child koalaed to my side
and that solid front porch within shadow

of the chestnut tree, its sticky blooms
each spring, spindly grenades come fall.

I am a stranger to those sweet anguishes
here—my spare western house

tucked up tight against its neighbors
in a bowl of shadeless avenue.

It helps to know the first house washed away
after we closed the front door

that its water broke
across the floors, flood ascending

and time stole back its offerings
by the hour we made land on this far shore.

The Quickening

Your first dreaming: Chicago,
nap in a hotel far away from your begetting.
Still, your beginning. Bubbles
down deep gurgling up
a tensile split at the top of me and you were real
at last. It felt like hiccups
but was really your ancestors
dragging a sun into your sky.
They set it against gray March
above exhalations and plumes
of midwestern work: my own begetting.
We are not a people
of songs and stories, so what
did they entrust to you, with what
did they lace your psyche
there by the lake
as I could only fathom
joy within?

Labor as an Exotic Vacation

Pretend it was a different adventure:
we traveled in our Chrysler down 8 Mile
as if in a dinghy, gliding
from the bright layer cake of yacht
toward an undiscovered port. Pretend
we were prepared for the awkwardness
of being foreign, seeking flimsy familiarity
and the perfect snapshot to send home.

We pictured white sheets and hand-holding,
new scenery and our faces changed.

But really it was like the tropics in July: sweaty
and panting, private and primal. Paradise
to one traveler can be hell for another,

so I won't bore you with the hours passed
watching the ocean swell and retreat,
the tall grasses bend and part in the wind
and some crazy, hooting monkey pulling itself up
impossibly straight tree trunks.

When we left at last we had a souvenir:
a golden idol shaped by heat,
meant to be worshipped.

Calendula

Through weed and tangle a flower at every portal:
tiny rings of fire expanding   then folding
each day with sun—these blooms,
their shatter of petals, needles of orange light, nothing
you can suture together
like a woman, like me:
small scar, single stitch I took
though we had anointed the doorway her body would make of me,
   we had traced it and traced it.
Not with blossom but its ointment,
which he, nothing else to do during the push,
applied to keep me from tearing. Oh well.
Here in the blazing garden,
lazy white mothdrift, roostercrow and bluster
all day long, I press a single bud
in the back of a book to preserve something:
its color maybe, its watery stalk. I pop
some leaves in my mouth to taste the name:
marigold, little calendar, weatherglass, clock
that ticked those hours and minutes,
the seconds and me
unfurling.   How I worked to open.

Nursing

See the pretty woman nodding?
See the pretty woman, skinny and blond, sharp
as youth, nodding.
See the man nodding?
The man who is also sharp
and handsome, too,
with crooked teeth.
See them nodding,
nodding over the cradle of a baby
and the baby a lump of light
cast up onto their faces, shadows
in their cheek hollows, heads nodding.

And when the man leaves the room
and the woman lifts her shirt,
see the dark coin of her nipple.
See the distended sack of breast
and the hungry mouth
like a buttonhole over it.
The woman nodding still
and see the man, the handsome man,
begin to enter and,
upon seeing the nipple almost swallowed
and no place for him on either side,
see him leave again.

Begin here: the baby
whose mother's breasts float above the cradle
like planets, whose mother's face
is the galaxy in which these planets move.
See the breast,
not its milk, not its steady stream
filling and heating the child,
but its endpoint, the origin
on which this baby's axis spins.

The nipple flops out glazed
in saliva and in purposeful point.
It is the breast that roots,
searches the tender face of the newborn, plumps
in her soft cheek seeking the mouth's
sweet suction.
  See the woman still nodding,
  the baby taking her mother in.

A Place, Asleep

For so long there was only fighting it:
she would cry and cry and we would stand
before this wailing as if before a tremendous fire
waving our hands, calling for helicopters,
shifting the weight of the world's sandbags between us
to stack and stack and stack them.
She consumed us, and we would sit in the wake
two scrappy pines uncurling amid ash and char,
occasionally disappointed we hadn't just burned up.

It isn't much better now. She's restless, doesn't want
to turn off this world that so delights
and seems to exist only for her. She sleeps eventually
and suddenly, spent like a match, drowsy flames
lazily lapping her toes as she surrenders to stubborn rest.

It is then I study her, sweet mouth open,
hands above her head like those first weeks we brought her home
and she would wriggle from her swaddling.
Always the arms above, reaching
for something she left in the other place,
something just hers. It isn't fair,
this world she makes herself in sleep,
this place we rush her to
but cannot follow.

Confession

In the chapel of our first days,
I put you to my breast again and again
and let you refuse me.

Half-life half-lived and with you
as my witness: I have been more
mother than woman. I have stayed up
all night lining the shelves of my life
with your toys and books.

It might be a comfort
the way my whole world spins
on the tip of your smallest toe,
but you will learn to be a woman
from the way I am a woman
in this world
and this is the litany
of my mistake.

Gone Song

Newly born, she slept
between us, fluttering and sucking:
a disembodied heart.
We crept downstairs
to make love. She is crucial
as lung, breath
more than limb
not quite brain. Before
she split me in two,
sloughed off my skin like a callus,
before she stood
or spoke
or wrote
she made her life
a leaving.

At the Monument

The girl has been upside down all day,
churning cartwheels and tipping up into handstands
in crosswalks, museum galleries,
the lawn of the National Mall. The fringe
of her suede jacket, a childhood relic my father
dug from his attic just last night, arcs behind her
like a single blade of pinwheel.

Soon she has decided to stage a photo,
lines herself up on hands beside the Washington Monument,
far enough in the foreground to appear
the same height—ramrod straight
with a splayed foot pierced
by the tower's peak.

In truth, I'm bored with this, distracted, caught
somewhere between childhood
and motherhood—shot after shot
and I can't get it right. A small flock
of sandaled tourists' gawks, one at last
grabbing my camera and throwing himself in the grass
to get the right angle.

Why can't I bring myself
to lie down on the lawn
for my daughter
when there's still so much
this love will ask of me?

She rights herself—
my camera floats back
and together we stoop curiously,
backs to the sun, admire
the her I hold in my hand.

Indication of Love

When I dropped her off at camp last week
she said, "Mom, just go,"
and wouldn't kiss me. I didn't think much of it
until later when I sat to work

and found her awkward 8-year-old scrawl
on the last pages of my notebook,
some school assignment, a description
of a painting in our house:

> *The way the feet are*
> *is the indication of love*
> *because the woman and the girl*
> *are holding hands*
> *but the woman is mostly behind.*

Domestic Short Hair

Lark of the open door and undetected flight.
If in truth this cat we found feral and shivering
has been somehow domesticated by our love,
then part of that is wanting this: escape,
another better lawn, a gang. We worry. The alley cats
howl outside our open windows.
They wait all year for something this good.

The cat teases us from beneath cars, flash
of tail around the side of the house. She is stray at heart—
clings to the edges of our yard
and refuses to reenter, refuses to fully flee.
She won't trade the glory of flight
for the bounty of return: small love
meted out weeknights when the dishes are clean,
the child asleep. Gone, she has every moment
of our worried attention. And also sardines,
a grown man prostrate and pleading,
a child beside him in tears: a duet
of pain and plot and plan.

And so I, too, call the name and click my tongue and wag
some piece of meat beneath the bushes and the porch.
I beg the cat to come home even as I wonder who we are
that know better than the animal what she needs.
I ask my husband what it is to domesticate
and demand loyalty in return.
I tell our daughter it will be OK.

Then I see the cat at last up close
and look into her cat eyes, still hungry
and wild with something to prove.
My husband, crooning and I-told-you-so,
said he knew she would come back. But I know better.
Left alone, she will never again walk through our door,
take her meal at our feet. It's force
in the end, the whole family trapping
and darting and flushing the thing out.

The Dead Thing

O effluvium of rat corpse, odor of mouse
droppings, funk from deceased bird. Niff
of decomposing squirrel; whiff of skunk.

Everywhere this smell of death—not a figurative
sense of doom pervading every thought,
but real—in every room putrid rot:

something has died in our ductwork.
O miasma of ancient raccoon jammed
between joists, fetor of possum or mole or maybe

the neighbor's lost cat.
The stink corrals us in a single room
we seal, infuse with incense,

windows open to morning mist
and autumn chill. For the first time
since our girl was a baby, the three of us

bed down and nest together,
the creaks and midnight stirrings of one
nudging us all in and out of uncomfortable sleep.

The perfume of our night sweat
mingles, a bouquet of hot breath
that fogs the vanity. Like a new litter

we weave together until we wake,
cranky and confined yet knit tight
against invading scent. O nothing lasts—good or bad.

So, come time: come you house flies
and scavengers, you insects, mites, beetles, larva,
maggots and worms: do your work.

Love, a Burnin' Thing

My daughter is giving up
on words—at least with me.
She slams the door,
berates me with silence.
I drop the needle on the record player,
hear Johnny Cash sing "Ring of Fire,"
and fall into that moment:
labor, one of the last times
an utterance adequately prepared me
for anything. How apt the phrase,
how perfectly rendered, how I felt
every centimeter ignited: my expansion
a perfect burning circle,
her soft skull crowned
in flare and flame.
Yes, the ring I slowly pushed
her through
toward oxygen
to kindle her breath.
Oh, how she wailed then
and we clung to one another,
all my knowledge
suddenly extinguished
as I listened to the certainty
of her voice:
knowing how I'd falter,
she was naming herself.

Palinode

I am not the one who cried on the airplane—it was only the baby beside me who sobbed and wriggled in his mother's arms, unable to find comfort.

I barely remember those days but that they were terrible, sweaty, her body against mine as I rocked and cooed and begged and whispered our secret language, her scent clinging to me, a mayfly.

I don't long for diaper bags, so many things to carry as I limped through the world, hobbled but prepared for anything.

I can no longer hear the echo: her shrieks from the backseat as I drove to daycare, which drove me to pull over and sob.

I don't crave the feeling of milk letting down hot like embarrassed blood when other babies cried.

Though I offered to hold him in our narrow row of seats so his mother could have a break, the bathroom by herself, it didn't make me pine for achy arms cradling her sleep while a dinner party dragged on down the hall without me.

I don't admire the stubbornness of babies, head shaking away a proffered pacifier, fat hands throwing soft silken blankets to the ground.

There were no moonless nights I'd usher out in streaky dawn, relieved I hadn't shaken her in fury.

And the weight of her between us in bed, the way she split our marriage neatly in half—before and after. Each day I'd wake to her pulling my nose, my hair, raising my eyelids. "Mama wake," she learned to say. Like a tyrant.

When the mother returned refreshed, arms open to receive the baby with a roll of her eyes, the grim face of duty, I didn't whimper like the baby when we separated, remembering my own chest atingle and cool in her absence when I would finally lay her down.

The only breasts to feed, the only voice and arms to soothe when there were others willing—I don't miss my body as her one relief.

Omne Trium Perfectum

Too alone we two were: a duet, tipping over
on our duo of shaky legs—
we needed another

to make us solid, triangular
like a milking stool, a trinity:
the many and infinite. Yes,

an oddness
but also indivisible
more practical than magical

(airplane row, circus rings,
pieces of suit), but
what ordinary magic!

Limit and goal, the start
of something: 1 . . . 2 . . .
3-legged race, a leap,

hands clasped, into the lake
and arc—not line—more fluid
than flat, more graceful

than straight. We are
excess and overflow:
waltz, polka;

not binary or system,
not symmetry,
not table, square, clout,

but something rare:
a curiosity. We are
braid, a weaving, a wisdom;

archetype and biblical, fairytale
tries or a coven
sharing a single eye.

We are danger,
too, in nature:
leaves of three.

Primary: all colors
can be made
from us, and all matter:

proton, neutron,
the swinging
electron: molecule

and elemental, two hydrogens
rounded by her oxygen, nothing
into water.

A bee
staggers out
of the peony

—MATSUO BASHŌ, TRANSLATED BY ROBERT HASS

Haibun at the Waterfall

The girl alone insists on swimsuit: mismatched with a bright orange bikini top, a little padded, and camouflage boy shorts, the whole getup gapey. Before breaching the water's cold skin, she hesitates at the edge, and I am a poor audience for her dramatics—swim away, the water a thousand iced tongues coaxing me from hot. Eventually she yelps, delights in the cool, soft embrace of the grotto, and before long she peels off her layers, is as naked as the moment she first slipped from me. I try not to openly marvel at her whole bare form for the first time in so long: swollen nubs of her nipples, new indentations and curves that tuck in just above her hip bones, dimply pudge that folds along her stomach's last remnants of baby fat, and is that a whisper of hair on her pubis? I can't let her see me staring, yet I can't help but stare. She seems to forget herself, her new self-consciousness, the way her body has betrayed her child-self by becoming something she's not yet ready to be. What pleasures will her body know, or does her body know already? How to ask: there is no way that is ours. I dive to the bottom in search of other treasures. She climbs deftly to the pools above the falls, her easy laughter trickling down. We remain alone, leaping from rocks in suspended time: no artifice, no hierarchy, no connection beyond spirit and body and now. Cold exposure breaks the spell. She reclaims and dons her suit, then a towel, then a haughty, embarrassed glance at my still-exposed breast. I cannot know when I will see her this way again, my once-other self. What changes will be wrought on her body I have loaned the world, which has already transformed it?

Pine siskin song
unzips greeny shadows:
a sound shift in light.

Morning Haibun with Tween

The girl can sleep now, hours and hours at a time—years since the last 2 am tiptoe down the hall to fold herself sweetly between us like a warm sheet. She sleeps now until noon if undisturbed, later even, forgoing the waking world while her body in sleep makes a woman. School days she sets an alarm, but it can't break the caul of her slumber—I crack the door, peel back the covers, count the minutes: *It's almost 7* I call, careful. Whether delay tactic or that her other self has fallen away, she is cuddles and sweetness, grasping for me, *I love you, Mama* in her soft low voice. *5 more minutes, please.* Sometimes I can't help it—I climb in the bed, look at the unguarded face, so ancient and dear and dangerous. Like looking at fire. And her hair, the feel of it as I brush, push it back from the sleeping countenance I have watched her whole life. When her eyes flutter open, it is to scowl at me, but when she rides again toward the crest of sleep, she burrows toward me: her first comfort. For a moment, I think to change her name to Sunshine, to Apple Blossom, to Beautiful Repose. But then she wakens, sour.

Oxalis, wood sorrel,
Bermuda buttercup:
Sunny flower, noxious weed.

The girl emerges from the bathroom wrapped in my new towel. *Hey, that one's mine* I say, surprised but not reproachful. *I thought yours was the tan one*, she says, holding the towel up tight against her new curves. She laughs a little as her long hair drips onto the hardwood and I catch my breath: this unfettered version so stunning. *I guess we've both been using that one,* I say. She pauses to decide how to react, and her body coils as if to fling the towel from it, her arm extending. *Eew!* she says, *You used this too?* surprised but not reproachful. She remembers her naked form beneath, snaps the towel shut, scurries to her room, and closes the door firmly. A moment later *Mom* she calls, the door open just one dark sliver and her thin, disembodied arm moving out through the crack, the towel pincered between the pads of finger and thumb as if it has turned rancid. *Here* she says as she drops it to the floor. The door closes again.

Deadheading spent blooms.
We once shared a body
now not even a towel.

The girl won't make her bus in time and a friend is waiting aboard. She should have to bear the consequences of not waking, I think. Still *I'll drive you to the bus stop,* I say. She rolls her eyes. *Fine* she says: the new gratitude. She scuffs into her shoes, flattening down the backs with her heels and then preemptive exasperation with what she thinks will be my protest: *I'll put them on in the car* she says. The digital clock on the dash is reproach. She looks at it and pouts *We'll never make it.* I want my daughter to be hopeful in this life, to persevere, to believe she has agency to do and be . . . but she's right: we see the bus cross several blocks in front of us and jet up the hill out of sight. Her defeated sigh. *We can catch it,* I say, gunning the engine. *Really?* she says: a glimmer. I turn sharply to speed up the hill and suddenly we are conspiracy, glancing at the end of each block for the bus we want to outrun. After a few blocks I realize I don't know the route: here is the part of her every day I know nothing of, cannot trace. *Go up two more blocks and right,* she says, scooting up in her seat, gripping the door, eyes shining. I gun again and swerve. She laughs out loud—it is almost a howl of delight.

Melon vines sprawl, need heat
to fruit. Soft, sweet flesh
& hard, mottled rind.

It is always the back of her I behold, can hold the longest. The girl gets out of the car, flips her backpack on one shoulder, slams the door and bites a quick *Bye* from the air, her back to me again. The bus kneels to her and she mounts it as on any other day, happy to greet the driver who was wondering where she was. Lights flash, slow growl of engine gathering momentum, my car in gear for the U-turn that will take me back down to where we started. And then suddenly her face through the scratched glass of the thick window, smiling and waving. We have come through the morning as if through clear water: I am drenched by it, but once dry, it will leave no mark.

Lilies of the valley &
forget-me-nots.
I gather and press.

Haibun in the Middle of the Night

Though she knows better the girl still says *nightmere,* a relic of early language when she also said *fleamingos* and *girled cheese.* Night*mere* as if to belittle: merely at night, merely a vision, and not some charging, lathered mare galloping through dreams to tear and divot the fragile terrain of sleep with rough-shod hooves. She holds on to this verbal tic and I my mother's ear, which hears her steps outside our room past 2 am, her tall 13-year-old body filling the doorframe and a whimper of explanation: *nightmere.* And so she logrolls between us stiff at first, no longer familiar with the sensation of family bed, sleeping between the two bodies that, in joy, made hers. Soon she curls toward fetal, her body's twitches a metronome to better dreams, her mind shifting to work that can't be done in the waking world. She rolls toward me, slings an arm around my waist and sighs.

Moon bright, surf roar, and
this rare touch—I can't
sleep from such delight.

Haibun with Norovirus

Just as I became accustomed to her new independence, her privacy, her one-word answers, the girl croaks "Mom!" early one morning from behind the bathroom door and I come to find her clinging to the lip of the toilet discharging a vomit so red and bright and brilliant it can't have been made by the body, and I remembered the way, just before bed the night before and against my objections, she had upturned a bag of XXtra Flamin' Hot Cheetos in her mouth. This vomiting is more than mere consequence, I can see, as her body works to purge itself entirely, throwing her head forward again and again.

Volcano spews lava,
bloodshot rock. I stand
astride it, my own force.

It will be like this for hours, each sip of water rejected, the very bile deep in the organs rejected, even thirst, hunger, the thought of food vomited up in dry yawps. In between the heavings, she will crumple to the bathroom floor, cool tile on her cheek, pale and weak, deflated, a raw little shrimp curled in pain. My body knows what to do. My body can give her body what it needs, older than instinct: I hold her hair as she vomits, I rub her back, I press cold compresses to her neck and forehead. In between, I rub her feet, cover her shivering body with a blanket, peel the covers back when she sweats. Like those early days when we nearly blew off our own roof with happiness, things are simple again, physical, a comfort I intuit and provide: need, survival. Her body tests limits but not her mouth—we barely speak beyond her complaints and moans, my assurances and coos. She squeezes my hand, I brush the hair from her eyes and forehead, an easy language. I draw a bath, I dry her off. She vomits more, I launder. I guide her to a nearby bed when she can trust her legs a few feet. She dozes. And like the infant mother I once was, I can tell when her sleep turns troubled, am there just before

she knows she has to lurch across the hall to kneel again. We pass an
entire day this way. I carry the water glass, I hold it to her lips.

Even suffering—
sweet lamb, Love, my honey pie—
has attendant joys.

Self-Defense Haibun

The school called it Assertiveness Training for girls 13 and over. At the end-of-day showcase they are practicing self-defense against their teachers who are disguised by inches of foam padding, blue mechanics overalls, and an alien-headed helmet with a narrow, deep slit at the eyes. It's a wonder these attackers can see and breathe and move at all, much less so deftly, one charging the girl with his arm raised in threat. An instructor in the corner yells, "Block that!" and the girl is motion, uses her arm to stop the figure in blue and pummels his chest with her fist. "Groin!" shouts the instructor, and the girl obediently executes. "Say No! Knee!" and the girl kicks and keeps punching and *no! no! no!*, a timid yelp.

Backyard birds skim
juniper, blossoms, the feeder:
never alight.

The blue figure keeps up the attack and begins to pat the places she should hit—a goading challenge. She unleashes herself, extends limbs from shoulder and hip stiffly, gives it everything she has. Then she screams louder, *NO! NO!* and hits wherever she can reach. Undeterred, he grabs her by the wrist and pulls her body to his body, turns her around, pins her arms, holds her back to his chest until she screams again, real this time. She kicks his knee and is free. But it isn't over. From behind, he sweeps her legs and is on top of her. I watch as breathless as the girl now wedged beneath him, shoulders pressed to the mat. "Eyes!" commands the instructor in the corner, and I realize mine are wet, that I am almost sobbing with this spectacle. Choreography so real, a relentless attack. As I despair she digs her thumbs into the slit of the helmet as if to gouge his eyes and is then on top of the man, banging his helmet into the floor *NO! NO!* kicking the groin, the knee, hitting the helmet until he falls back for good and it is over and everyone calls "Good job."

Poison berry, potential
weapon: to be woman,
to know violence.

Haibun on the Ides of March

The Ides of March have come but not gone and we are in the car on the way to school. The girl is crying again, cannot catch her breath or remember how or why, only that she is angry and I am the problem. There are times these days I wish for something impossibly dramatic—a piano or anvil to disgorge itself from sky, perhaps, and land beside us—rather than continue this infinity of quarrel: who won't listen or love, who doesn't understand, who can't be bothered to pick up her socks from the living room floor. Who is this child beside me, railing against each word, hurling insults until I, too, begin to weep? *You are horrible*, she says, *I hate you*. And it's not as if I hold my tongue, laced more with pain than poison. We are a wild, primal thing. I want to fling myself from the car, she wants to fling me from the car, but we both need me to keep my hands on the wheel steady in traffic, ignoring glances from drivers to our left and right—this is none of their business. Listen: I am no Caesar, need no lifelong crown. To say a girl must overthrow her mother to make her way as a woman is absurd. Yet as she winds up again in fresh attack, *You never, you always, I can't stand*, I wonder if she'd thrill to see me conquered on the marble stair, or even just this dashboard, so she can rise to rule, her own Octavius.

Crow feather and strife
so common we learn to praise
not to bury them.

Sweet and Fitting Haibun

Bent double, cinched in contraction and blind with anticipation
I labored to bring forth her tiny body till on the safe and ordered
world of hospital we turned our backs and trudged toward life
without rest. Drunk with joy we survived night feeding and weaning,
through tummy time and temper tantrum to the ecstasy of late
toddlerhood: some independence, easy laughter, deep devotion.
Hung like twin planets in her consciousness, we were gravity,
inspiration, divinity. Not soldiers but soldiering. There was rapture
in years six and seven, in her spunk and clever wit, and then some
sass at eight or nine we weathered. It's not the same as war, I know;
I do not suffer as one gassed, but when the hormones dropped like
bombs and the outside world seeped in at last, she began to turn
from me. I faltered in my advance, walked around aflame with
adolescence. Her easy dismissal pierced my heart's weak shield and
battlement but was no preparation for full assault: rage at nothing,
pure hatred's countenance, impatience with my very breath and
speech. What could I do? I folded my dreams in her lunchbox and
slipped her a ten-dollar bill. Soon there will be curfews and half-
truths, maybe some nudes, beer or weed on her breath, a piercing
or tattoo. If someone had told me I would become, like my own
mother, bug-eyed and impatient, a traitor to my own intention;
if someone had told me I would walk straight into a wall where I
thought there was none; if someone had told me I'd sometimes rather
chew off a limb than endure, well even then I would beg them tell
me the old lies: that it goes so fast, that it gets easier, that it's worth it,
sweet and noble, in the end.

Morning dews each day.
Still the sun sets on horror
as it does on joy.

My body broke when the bees left,
became a thing of bones
and spaces and stretched skin.

—JO SHAPCOTT, "CCD"

Collapse

What do bees want? is a question I've never asked
myself or any expert. I know they need

to gather pollen & nectar, need water & shelter,
though they can make their own of any hollow place.

But as to *want*, who can say? I say
I need to take my vitamins, apply sunscreen,

eat greens & exercise—want self-care, something
I deserve (for what I do not know).

Our bodies are built to decay. I opened
the hive only as often as I was told:

to check brood, the health of the queen.
I did not know what I was looking for but trusted

diligence would keep us from disaster.
They wanted me out of their way,

so I closed it all up,
left them to their own desires.

3585 Mission Street San Francisco CA

Unpacking new apartment
new city I was distracted
in the kitchen when I heard the shatter
the tinkling glass
and saw my daughter up against
the broken window
having stumbled into and somewhat out of it
her backside hanging out over the street
so I leapt the boxes
grabbed her soft arms hard
hauled her back how had I not seen
the danger of those windows
we were drawn to at the Open House
single-paned floor-to-ceiling their whole-body sweep
of Twin Peaks the daily fogcreep
the traffic and palm trees that line Dolores Avenue
to where it ascends out of view
and though the place wasn't perfect
not Victorian not brightly colored
no stained glass or hardwood floors
it came with a garage and rent control
access to the backyard and
this new world that almost took her
that very first day but I didn't see
a bad omen didn't let it
change our course we had
good years at the table we placed there
and while we dined we could lean out and see it all
drunk driving checkpoints
that lit up our white walls red and blue
annual barefoot pilgrimage
parishioners carrying their Mary aloft
and even fireworks

when July fog wasn't so thick
we could only feel their thuds in our chests
those constellations illuminating the pale green building
caked with road dust and street grime
and the foreboding iron gate
visitors would pass through
to come upstairs and say wow that view
which I loved
until those endless days
after we replaced the table with a couch
and I was pinned to it
hoping the poison in my veins would cure me
so sick I could barely lift my head
to watch the orange-gold sun dip
beneath the peaks and the sky
would stain so bright my skin
in reflection looked like fire itself
and I wonder now if those windows
were a curse from the very beginning
that I didn't heed
or if they were my bit of salvation.

Melanoma

The speck could have been the footprint
of a tiny god alighting on my shoulder
but instead is devil—his blackened eye,
harbinger, new moon, bottomless well. Will I too
be brought down by a sliver
of vulnerable flesh? Cup of midnight
spilled where I cannot reach, errant
mole, black hole, darkened window opening
onto Death's back porch. So much battle
left in me but for this chink in the armor,
fingerprint of destruction, fatal kiss,
burnt tip of match just touched to the pyre.

After the Phone Call I Teach Book 11

You're Odysseus, or you're dead:
some forgotten bit of flotsam
left to die along the way. Fate
is absolute, and I've taught this book so long

there is no other way to hear
the news on the phone
when the doctor calls before class
with biopsy results.

My 9th graders file into our room
and I am at the whim of divine irony:
my mortality unspooling
just as I have to teach a lesson

on Odysseus' journey to the Underworld
where he hears true suffering
isn't the moment of death
but the endless afterlife.

Of Achilles' monologue
one student opines
even the worst life
is better than the best death. Can this be true?

Achilles would rather be a slave on earth,
breathing fresh air, suffering
adjacent to a living happiness,
instead of turning in fields aglow with asphodel.

Odysseus, too, chooses his human body.
Offered immortality, a gorgeous goddess,
life of pleasure, he will yearn
for home instead, beset as it is with uncertainty

and so many threats of death. My students
need to believe there are things worse
than the capricious gods of adolescence
playing their hearts like strung lyres,

even if it's just death. But I want to quibble
with Achilles: it isn't any life that's better.
It's mine.
It's my life that needs to be saved.

Insomnia

All night my fear like a candle
not bright enough
or hot enough
to do much damage
but ambient
flickering and spitting
a thick wisp of black smoke
licking the ceiling:
dreams of my undoing.

Tumor Board

World without absolutes:
                            just waiting,
a wilderness with as many guides as paths
and still just one Charon
plunging his pole again and again into forgetfulness
to pull the vessel across.

And these doctors:
there is nothing else
to cross their palms with, no vapor
from deep crevices of earth
that will let them riddle out my future: it is all
conjecture and no emotion,
Data the only temple.

I am not the earth
rotating through its seasons: they
will tell me if it's spring or winter.

Would they ask their wives, I wonder,
to follow this slick path they've pointed me down
toward the very dark mouth of hell
and turn back just in time to deposit myself
into some sunny field of flowers?

Of course they would.

And I will do what they tell me. Trust
has no place in the conversation.

They are not gods, they are not godly, but
I still wait all week
for them to classify this blossoming,
to measure out some length of thread
I'm not meant to see until it snaps.

Postcard to My Left Axillary Lymph Nodes

Dear friends:

It's my third year here in this limbo, where I wonder each day
if an errant cell slipped your filtery grip and vesseled along
the vast highway to colonize a distant organ. But the weather
has been fine—so many Kool-Aid-colored sunsets to drink in
as I learn the tyranny of treasuring every moment. The food:
exquisite—I ate some sort of broth last week that barely
made me think of first days without you, recording every drop
of amber fluid from surgical drains. Tomorrow I will jump on
a trampoline or have a massage to drain some swelling from
my arm. I miss your glandular protection, little nodes tucked
up in me like a charm in a pocket. Wish you were here!

Curls

For a year I took poison,
let every part of me suffer
to root out a conflagration of cells.
Some cure.

The body holds grudges:
bruises for small jostlings,
scars to mark larger transgressions.
Its language is exact
and exacting:
cellulite and stretch mark,
sunspot, mole, lump and nodule,
worn-out joints and leaky valves. We struggle
against embodiment,
age and decay a revenge
for not yet finding
                    the immortal path.

When my body let me have my hair again,
it came back curled:
calyxed and spiraled,
unrecognizable each time
my reflection surfaced in a window,
a mirror above the sink,
a photo on your phone: how I circled

back to harm on a loop,
a carousel of anguish
I wear now to frame my new face,
its creases and bloat:
my body keeping track
of what I've done to it.

The Last CT Scan

Strange comfort:
 almost-divine

glimpse at organs
 and systems

deep bones
 and crevices

 never meant for human eye.
There will be no more tangible

no more barium
ease of IV needle in vein,

 of drugs
lighting the path:

bioluminescence striking aglow
 against organs and growths.

 Let there be no more
of this trauma and threat:

series of closed doors
 and no windows

hallway clogged with gurneys
 whisper of booties/bodies

hope or fear
 an opening I slip through

back and forth
again and again

holding my breath, releasing
 my breath. Still.

Farewell image of torso
        blooming suddenly on the small screen

melanin ink exploding
        in the tank

curiosity and wonder:
        my undulations inside.

Gratitude

Don't talk to me of a god:
it's not what saved me.

(And it's not what unleashed profligate cells:

       punishment   warning.)

Not just soul I am

a concrete form:

      text
              vehicle
                    matter.

So I say my prayer

to the lungs

        each day unconsciously expanding

my trunk a bellows of effort

          each nave of me replete.

I thank
      this institution
           of self:

   corporeal   incarnate frame

muscles that lift my body

    from the bed   to the couch   to the world

that beat my heart

and turn my head toward sunlight:

      the aggregate

the ocean of fluids:

      blood   lymph   urine   bile

tide of systems pumping

      T cells and lymphocytes   principal and material

           (they take my health
           where it is needed).

Celestial and

      resonant

      while holding back the darkness:

I thank nothing

      but my body
      for this life.

Found Notebooks Haibun

On my way out the door to a meeting I grab any old notebook
from the shelf so I seem prepared. I assume it blank, but it is full of
numbers: Nate's careful scrawl and lists of measurements: date, time,
milliliters—a liquid timetable of those first weeks home with our
daughter who wouldn't latch, who was, the lactation counselor told
me, *failing to thrive*. We went home with an industrial breast pump,
a milker: a whirring, squeaking box of suction whose sounds I still
lose in the memory of baby coos and exhalations. I clamped myself
in every hour while she squirmed and screamed in Nate's arms, and
when I was done, I would trade him: baby for the bottles fresh from
the pump. He would carefully hold them up to the light and measure,
recording every mL of the golden fluid that we dropped into the
mewling hole of her uncooperative mouth. And later scatological
reporting from the changing table—so much detail and excitement,
our world shrunken to charting each molecule as it passed from me
through her.

Lake's deepest point is black,
difficult to fathom:
love's devotion.

Packing for our move, I mistake a notebook for the one we kept
when our daughter was born: those martyred measurements. But it's
a different liquid record—still Nate's writing, military and precise
with measurement, but the liquid is lymph: sticky, smelly, never-to-
be-seen fluid leaking from me after all my nodes were removed. This
lymph pooled in plastic surgical drains that Nate emptied, I read,
on 2/14 at 1:40 am, 8am, 12 pm, 4pm, 9pm, 12am. For days he kept
this record of walking me to the bathroom, unpinning the small
balloons of bloody bodily syrup and dumping the contents into a
measuring cup we still use in the kitchen today. He measured with
his scientist's eye and recorded 40 mL, 12 mL, 3 mL, 7mL, watching
the measurements fluctuate as my body adjusted to the new blocked

pathways and swellings. No one told him to do this. No one was waiting for the data. Who even asked him?

Rain gauge measures
what falls from the sky.
What quantifies survival?

Tattoo Artist

When the young girl wants my input

On the design of her tattoo

The bells of my brain don't know

Which alarm to sound first

I am her teacher her father

Is my friend she babysits my daughter

Her mother is days away from dying I think

Perhaps I should dissuade her though

Part of me thinks to cheer I want

To know the right advice to give but what

Does it matter she's already marked

And the dull buzz of the tattoo gun

Will be in her ears always the needle

Piercing her flesh will be nothing

Like the pain that traces itself each day

Through her heart

What is ankle bone shoulder blade

Hip skin over the kidney why not

Wear pain permanently

An heirloom brooch I would

Turn up her sleeve myself

If I could I would dip into each colored well

And puncture her skin again again

With what very little I know of loss.

Diagnosis

It is not yet the last burger
you will ever taste. And the walk
around the cul-de-sac is not the last time
we will admire the black tree raised like a fist
against a wide-open autumn sky.

Nor do we speak in firsts:
first thought after
the pronouncement. First peek
at the calendar, calculating.

In fact we cannot speak at all, pilgrim
our way to the craft store instead
and stock your cabinets with yarn enough
for a hundred lives: great balls of it, masses,
small clouds billowing, lawns of it,
soft knots of it, fleshy some of it,
coarse and rough some.

                        One day
I will find these skeins unused
and gather them to me like children.
I will name them what they might have been:
Sweater. Scarf. Blanket. Cowl. Mitten.

I will not think of them
as *first* or *last* or even *if.*
It will just be a sort of *yes,*
you were here. For a while
you lived.

I Make Us Watch *America's Got Talent*

so we can use up all our tears.

You say it's cheap. Emotional drive-thru.
You say it's designed to provoke.

I say

Show me guitar-playing soldiers
still jaunty on prosthetic legs.
Give me arias from single mothers,
dancing toddlers, magic acts,
wayward teens redeemed
on flaming pogo sticks:

I'll weep.

You'll thank me tomorrow, love,
getting chemo in that easy chair.
We'll have more to talk about
than what's snaking up your spine,
and I'll be all cried out:

I'll be fine. I'll be fine.

At the End

I slept all night in the chair beside you.

The nurse dimmed the lights, showed me how to recline.

There were no machines beeping.

Before going home to bed, my sister reached down and pulled your eyelids back, showed how the pupils wouldn't focus.

I knew I was there for myself.

All night we circled.

Your breath would pause a beat too long, and I would rise straight up, some stepped-on rake, my face in yours.

Then you would inhale: sharp, sudden.

You kept breathing, mouth a tiny, perfect oval, slightly beaked.

I put my hands on your legs as they grew colder.

Day broke and still you breathed.

They had said an hour once the tubes were out, but I counted at least twenty.

My sister returned and hadn't missed much.

We sat together, the two of us chatting beside your bed, eating breakfast.

Then she got up to leave for work.

One more breath and it was over.

They left me alone with your body.

Next Lines

After the last breath, calm.
There are papers to sign and stamp,
plans to put in place. Turn off
the thermostat, unplug the lamps.
The night's labor was long but the day new,
everything backward and beautiful.
It will keep. Go outside,
plant flowers she would have liked
in her favorite pot. Mow the lawn.
Weed the bed, wrestle
the hose from the garage—it's time
to help the season work its magic:
count the promise of apple blossoms,
inhale the decay of warming mulch.
Make note: this audacity
won't last long.

Elegy

There is nothing new to say about love.
When I last slept next to you
I dreamed a newborn with your voice
talked to me about it
as I held and nursed her. My body
is always looking
for new ways to contain you.

It's easy to make a metaphor of death—
rotting corpse and carriage ride, stealthy
robber bee, stubborn, pouting child.
What I miss most are the meals: steak
with melted butter, French-cut beans,
our own cartons of vanilla ice cream. Your hunger
at the end as wide as the sky in drought.

At the Memorial Service

Through the windows, Bay and Bridge,
a panorama from the city's ragged edge
all the way to Treasure Island.

Glinting windshields rush and flash above,
while on the lower span
shadowy trucks trudge away.

A few white caps betray the volatile tide
and a fierce trawler struts by. Behind
the first to stand and speak, a container ship—

brightly colored cargo stacked up neat—
slowly unfurls, letter by letter, its starboard name:
China Shipping Line. The words we hear

have no bearing on the weather, yet
we note when gray abates and sun
calls passengers on passing ferries out to deck.

The bridge holds a looming belt of clouds at bay
and the brighter the day grows,
the more silhouetted the voices.

Muteness rises and falls
as unpredictably as gulls.
A few sobs, some muffled comfort.

One terrific barge, no cargo, no purpose
to the cables strung across the gunwales,
chuffs along, kicking up some cursory bit of foam.

And then the piano, tucked as if beneath
the bridge's unseen first approach,
stands up in quiet melody.

We are left with the man-made island on one side,
city nestled on the other, chasm of sea,

the bridge now choked with traffic.

Aubade in the Hour Between

Dawn's edge of fitful night and I
am almost waking still asleep
beside her propped on pillows
in her own bed her own room
making jokes of my concern or

                                she is walking
down the drive hands jammed in pockets
dog on her heels while I am in the circle waiting
beneath apple blossoms I am drunk with scent
she has something to say there is something
delicious on the stove it is

                        the hour of possibility
a house where I want to live
I think we are out of eggs or bananas—I need to
run to the store before breakfast
there is still so much to do to be ready
but we are busy turning up the earth
in her perennial garden *Your lupine or your life*
she says as she unpots and tears at roots to bury
and didn't the forecast say
thunderstorms so why all this Wedgewood blue sky
and the rattle of china in the cabinet as neighbors
open their garage the noise
of someone else's machines breathing
and beeping through the wall all night
I am wearing one of the starched Easter dresses
she smocked by hand or her hospital gown
I am mapping her wrinkles as she sleeps
did I set the alarm?
I want to sketch the oval shape of her mouth
as it rasps her last air I say "Open your eyes"
and she sticks out her tongue

                        maybe it's a joke

then the cat's steady meow from the kitchen
my bladder's tug
sunlight's bright announcement
climbing the walls
and the horn falls off the unicorn
the world is fully a horse now
and she is gone from it.

Everything Is a Sign Today

Feather in the grass, stippled and striped:
hawk, I think. And then a man
blocking the sidewalk, child on his back,
both of them pointing binoculars toward the treetop
where I know a great horned owl nests, though I've never seen it.
All these birds: creatures I might never have known
had I not spent my childhood filling her feeders, naming
each genus from our perch at her kitchen table.
A falcon swoops down beside me on the path
gripping some rodent in its talons, twisting the body to kill.
Like the time a heron a few feet from our picnic blanket
plucked a whole mouse from its burrow and swept away. She had been
delighted, said we, too, should grab something special
of our own that day. Turning toward home,
I bend to collect a wrinkled postcard at the curb:
an advertisement for the Monet exhibit. How I loved
those paintings when I was younger, all of them nearly the same:
haystack, haystack, haystack. The only difference
the season and time of day, which is to say
they are like this grief these months later:
all the same but for the light.

Fame is a bee.
It has a song—
It has a sting—
Ah, too, it has a wing.

—EMILY DICKINSON, 1788

Afterswarm

As for when my first bees knit themselves together
in a single sovereign self and slunk over the fence
in search of their truant queen, I couldn't say—
not with my own house to mind.

They could have been gone for weeks
when I noticed the hive grave-still
and empty of their chants.

By then, a thing inside me, some rotten cell,
had broken off, too, though I didn't yet know
it was sliding through a dark body system,
the same stealth path as swarm, a channel
not meant to be traced by eye or dye
until arrival: seething growth
suspended low.

Though I looked, I didn't find my missing bees,
a fist of them dangling from a neighbor's tree
excised from the world, their hive left full of labor—
I couldn't call them home.

What an easy harvest!
My first, no need to leave honey
so bees could overwinter, measuring
enough for me, enough for them.
I cut wax caps from cell tops,
spun out every drop
and took it all.

Now this last jar, all grit and crystal with age.
It's time to order a new batch of bees for spring,
clean the moldy hive brought down from rafters
and brush out my veil.

I will be alive this time
to what swells and roils the colony, the first cluster
gathering on the fence line. I will heed.

Bad at Bees

Aganetha Dyck is an artist who puts broken figurines and tchotchkes in hives for her bees to mend: a collaboration. The objects come out with honeycomb in place of chipped rims, missing limbs, fractured edges.

I think my husband hoped this second round of bees, a gift for my birthday, would do the same for me—knit around the hole the first hive left when it swarmed away some years back, right as I got too sick to notice.

My favorite Dyck piece is a figurine of three people in Georgian dress, their bodies transformed: two women's wigs honeycombed and heightened, chairs ballooning behind them like giant wings or a tsunami mounting, about to sweep them away. The comb binds them together with a thick single leg beneath the table, slickens the surface of the checkerboard on top. The pantalooned man leaning over is flounced and ruffled in comb, a new arm of clean hexagon extending from his shoulder around one of the skirted ladies.

I want to ask my bees to fix the handmade bowl I splintered, but I've been afraid to crack the lid since they arrived and I installed the nucleus. I can't even bring myself to remove the queen cage I left dangling between frames once the bees chewed through the sugar plug to extract her. That alien piece of furniture is probably messing up what is called "bee space" in the new architecture of the hive, where workers should be pulling comb straight and making an order of things.

One morning I did try to get in there and have a look. It didn't go well.

When I called my sister later to confess what a bad beekeeper I am, she just said, "Wait, tell me again what you were wearing." I had only thought to open things up and finally get the cage out when I came back from surfing still in my wetsuit and realized that, even though it's black and you're not to wear dark clothing when tending a hive lest the bees think you a bear, they probably can't sting through neoprene. Without much thought I threw on my veil and went to the hive.

I don't usually smoke my bees and couldn't find my gloves, but I forged ahead anyway, inspired by an essay by a beekeeping poet I adore who says he goes to his bees in thin-soled shoes, gloveless and shirtless, vulnerable so they know he isn't there to harm them.

But that isn't what my sister wanted to know about. "So you were wearing a wetsuit and a bee veil?" she asked. "Did anyone see you?"

Of course I hadn't really thought of that because once I opened the lid, I realized I was in over my head—the bees had begun to build comb all around the empty queen cage. The frame was combed onto others when I tried to scooch it out to take a look. When I lifted it up, the peaceful chants and hums of the hive increased exponentially to a sort of roar. I could feel the heat of bee bodies radiating, and the sudden gap meant they could hurl themselves up in the air and scatter around me. I lost my nerve and set the frame down quickly, righted and closed everything up, but not before a bee stung my unprotected thumb.

Thank goodness it was on the side of my body where I hadn't had to have all my lymph nodes removed. I'm not supposed to sustain even a scratch on that hand, much less a puncture wound—no IVs or blood pressure cuffs, though I don't exactly know what would happen.

I got the stinger out right away, its venom sac still attached and pulsating, my thumb so swollen I couldn't hold a pen for two days while I alternated ice, Advil, and Benadryl to relieve the pain, swelling, and itching.

I didn't even go surfing like I usually do, although I don't use my thumb much in the water—the sting was just an excuse because the week before all this bad bee business I had some bad ocean business.

It was my first real scare out in the winter swell, and I wasn't eager to return to that huge body of water, where I had been caught far outside the break and separated from my mat in heavy surf. I tried to swim to shore, but each wave swallowed me, pulled me back, under, upside down no matter how I worked to bodysurf or duck it.

Panicking, not getting any closer to the beach, running out of breath, I was feeling pretty stupid—like, is this really the way I'm going to die after everything else? At last my foot hit sand and I realized I would make it, but I got right out and rode my bike home fast as I could in case the ocean wasn't done with me, its long arms reaching to pull me back in on a sneaker wave.

When the new beekeeping gloves I ordered get here, I'm not going to mess around anymore—I'll suit up and crack that hive open to fix it all up.

But I'm not going to make a regular habit of it or anything. I'll hack the queen cage from the comb where the bees have ensconced it in their craft and just leave them alone for a few months to get settled, make some brood and honey. I trust they will forgive me, find a way to rebuild, mend my destructive path through their ordered home.

And while it may not be a figurine, my handmade bowl, or some tchotchke enhanced by carefully constructed creamy comb, I'll place the queen cage and what's attached to it on my writing desk. Maybe it will inspire a new way to think about containment, my human form. And maybe some mornings it will make me close up my desk and get back in the water.

I hope no one will see it there and ask me about it, though, because I hate how I sound when I say things like "Yeah, I keep bees in my backyard," or "Yeah, I surf most mornings," "Yeah, I'm a poet," as if I'm any good at any of it. I don't really know what I'm doing most days. I just like to touch fear.

ACKNOWLEDGMENTS

Grateful acknowledgment to the readers and editors of the anthologies and journals where these poems, sometimes in different forms, first appeared.

All We Can Hold: Poems of Motherhood, "At the Monument"

Ambush Review, "Waggle Dance"

Bared: Contemporary Poetry and Art on Bras and Breasts, "Nursing"

Cave Wall, "20905 Caledonia Avenue Hazel Park MI" and "Tumor Board"

Coal Hill Review, "Foraging"

Coe Review, "Ithaca"

The Cortland Review, "Sonnet While Killing a Chicken," "Anniversary Declaration"

Cream City Review, "Opening the Hive"

Eastern Iowa Review, "Haibun in the Middle of the Night"

Glass: A Journal of Poetry, "Confession"

Grist: A Literary Journal, "Calendula"

The Greensboro Review, "Requeening"

Hartskill Review, "I Make Us Watch *America's Got Talent*"
  Mamas and Papas: On the Sublime and Heartbreaking Art of Parenting, "Clementine Asleep"

NELLE, "Morning Haibun with Tween"

Nostos, "Haibun at the Waterfall," "Haibun in the Middle of the Night," "Found Notebooks Haibun"

Pidgeonholes, "Found Notebooks Haibun"

Potomac Review, "At the Monument," "Diagnosis"

Sequestrum, "Elegy"

Sixfold, "Tattoo Artist," "The Dead Thing"

Sweet: A Literary Confection, "Which Came First"

SWIMM Every Day, "Labor as an Exotic Vacation" "My Life Still with Wasps"

Tahoma Literary Review, "The Broken Leg"

THAT Literary Review, "Aunt Annie's Sand"

Typehouse Literary Magazine, "Curls"

What We Talk About When We Talk About It: Variations on the Theme of Love, "Indication of Love"

The Writing Salon, "When I Hear 'Horses' as 'Corsets'"

ZYZZYVA, "Collapse," "Domestic Short Hair"

Many poems, fragments, and ideas from this book have benefited, as have I, from the support, reading, and attention of people to whom I am deeply grateful. I will certainly fail in listing everyone who has touched my life and influenced this work, but my gratitude is nevertheless profound. I would like to expressly thank the following people:

Ocean Vuong, not only for choosing this manuscript, but for the light you shine in the poetry world and beyond, helping so many of us find our way. Reading you and being read by you has transformed me.

My early writing teachers who believed in my work and showed me a path to it: Robert Marrs, Gordon Mennenga, Wendy Bashant, Ken McLane, and Archie Ammmons among them.

Gabriella Doob and the whole team at Ecco, including Elizabeth Yaffe, Christina Polizoto, David Stanford Burr, Martin Wilson, Paula Russell Szafranski and the many whose names I don't know who nevertheless labored to bring this book to print.

Director Beth Hicks, engineer Patrick Fitzgerald, and executive producer Suzanne Franco Mitchell, who made recording the audiobook such a thoughtful and enlivened experience, revealing to me new ways to hear and understand my work.

The teachers and workshop groups who have welcomed and educated me, including Cornell University's MFA program; the Minnesota North Woods Writing Conference and Aimee Nezhukumatathil, who urged me to find a floating feather in my haibun and was the first to remind me that, because hives collapse, there was room for those poems in this collection; the Tin House Summer Writing Workshop and Maureen McLane for her guidance, good humor, and generosity; and the Napa Valley Writers Workshop and Eavan Boland.

Ellen Bass and the amazing women in her Wednesday Workshop Group, who have taught me where the heart of poetry lives while providing me with inspiration and feedback.

David St. John, Susan Terris, and the Cloudview Poets, who have so warmly embraced and encouraged me.

The Writing Salon for honoring me with the Jane Underwood Prize, the San Francisco Writers Grotto for their support through the Grotto Fellowship Program, and The Ruby for space and time.

Daniel Handler and Lisa Brown for their vision and support, along with the Friends of the San Francisco Library Staff and my amazing Brown Handler Residency cohort, whose commitment to their own work and our shared community was inspiring.

In Cahoots Residency for the sublime space to organize and complete this manuscript with the support of Macy Chadwick and her magical menagerie.

My students, friends, and colleagues at the Urban School of San Francisco, whose talent and vision motivate and inspire me every day. Special gratitude to my officemates, my group text threads, and the administrators who have helped me strike a balance that honors teaching and writing.

Rebecca Foust, for her counsel and sharp editorial eye, and all the poets who have let me learn from and write about their poems for Women's Voices for Change Poetry Sunday.

Nina Riggs, who inspired and helped me find the courage to write some of the hardest poems in the book; she was their first reader and supporter.

All the poets I am lucky enough to have learned from and with, who have gifted me with their readership, friendship, and insight, including Sarah Audsley, Joseph Campana, MK Chavez, Carrie Rice Gardner, Nancy Miller Gomez, Ken Hass, Amanda Hawkins, Maria

Carlos Isabelle, Danielle Janess, Janet Jennings, Siân Killingsworth, Ruby Hansen Murray, Meryl Natchez, Yamini Pathak, Erin Redfern, L. Renee, Barb Reynolds, Molly Spencer, Maw Shein Win, and Crystal Williams.

My friends, who have encouraged and sustained me in myriad, unnamable, and profound ways over the years; trekked to attend my poetry readings; cared for me and my family; and served as models for living lives of love and generosity, including Sandra Beaudin, Karen Capraro, Zoe Christopher, Sydney Cohen, Angela Eaton, Nick Davis, Karen Hand, Cyd Harrell, Ellen Hathaway, Johnathan Howland, Laura and David Lamberti, Riley Maddox, Greg Monfils, Charles Moré, Julian Morris, Courtney Rein, Andy Rivera, Kristie Rudolph, Dave Smith, Jennifer Starkweather, Angela Wall, and Crystal Williams.

Joseph Campana, Molly Spencer, and Barret Warner, who each went above and beyond to help me fashion this manuscript from raw material; loved, supported, and challenged it; and are indelibly a part of what it has become.

The Pacific Ocean and my steady morning companions: dolphins, seals, Anthony Consilio, and John Webb.

Judy Kearns, whose lessons guide me through most days.

The incredible women of my family, who have provided me with comfort, joy, and so many stories, including Genevieve Moore, Frances Reed, Linda Reed, and K.C. Ipjian, the ultimate worker bee. Gratitude as well to John and Mary Moore.

Nate Nelson, who has walked with me and held me through lightness and darkness for over half my life, whose care and support make everything I do possible.

My daughter, Clementine, my brightest thing.

NOTES

"1729 Maple Avenue Northbrook IL" borrows its anaphoric "Gone" from the first stanza of Crystal Williams' poem "Detroit as Barn."

"Love, a Burnin' Thing" takes its title from a lyric in Johnny Cash's song "Ring of Fire," which is further referenced in the poem.

"Sweet and Fitting Haibun" borrows part of its title from Horace by way of Wilfred Owen's "Dulce et decorum est," which, translated from the Latin, means "It is sweet and fitting to die for one's country." My poem further references and borrows elements from Owen's poem.

"The Tattoo Artist" is for Madeleine.

NOTES